DEAD WINTER

DEAD WINTER
Matvei Yankelevich

FONO
GRAF

FONOGRAF EDITIONS

Fonograf Editions
Portland, OR

Cover and text design by Mike Corrao

First Edition, First Printing

FONO19

Published by Fonograf Editions
www.fonografeditions.com

For information about permission to reuse any material from this book,
please contact Fonograf Ed. at info@fonografeditions.com.

Distributed by Small Press Distribution
SPDBooks.org

ISBN: 978-1-7344566-9-1

∇

Winter comes calling while I'm on
vacation, auto-responder,
et cetera — the book's not done,
mail piled like snow. Of a sudden
life looks brief, just *this mangled foam,*
this form for which you've spared no part —
there might not be a chance to change
or quit changing. My blue notebook's
sad and modern. So, if I write
the self is wispy — sure, but, strike
that line. They say you can't edit
poetry, but I say, fuck it.

Spring snow or winter doesn't know
when to go. Dogs are like kids or
the other way. Wonder around
leaving more out. Or most of it.
But then why elevate what's left
to music? Poetry's no more
than genre, avant-garde's a style —
they've got horror/sitcom poems
at a bargain. I don't buy me —
another genre; try it on
for size. That shackles make a self,
some jailbreak need to feel it chafe.
Can you get to what? Go 'head,
get down while I get under it.

∇

My task, my cross — to reassemble winter's
memory? Each fingernail, each checker
on my shirt, each knot of knits, each follicle,
and every cone? — Doors shut at my enquire,
forgetting of when was it we first met.
Why ask for closure, when there's nothing final?
The BBS is down. Cursive's untaught...
Yet I taste the iron in the walnut.
Because I read so little and so slowly,
turns bend now only to who I was again,
appear as habit. Widely believed to have
writ adverse advices for adulterers,
I scour notebook prose for hidden meters,
my flaws dressed up as inconsequent failure,
crime camouflaged in error. Tell me now
the course, poor navigator, to the shore.

Winter's prison: fog, the titles I write down to read,
each night too short to write that letter you would rather
I not write. Here useless struggle's worth my while, I cleave
persistent loafing, desperate inertia. To sing
without a tune, figuratively abstract: the sound
product of tying my shoes. Now, when I'm pulsed to change
a word, I often leave it, not — my suspicious friend —
for love of it as is, but of serious boredom,
so that you too may feel that drag, and this hang, also.

On winter's hungry mornings, bloated belly and weak joints,
I tried writing it down, putting it down and expressing
what was inside and getting it out, setting it down, and
drawing it out of me, adding to it, sculpting from it
like a slab, stabbing, chiseling away, hammering blows,
making a hole in myself from which it could flow like paint,
making an opening, and beating the rhythm out of
sentences, and breaking it down, abandoning it to
fester and foam as puss out of the wound and down onto
the page (down being the direction), out onto the page
(out being the direction), pushing it, expelling it
outward toward the page (being the direction), describing
it as best I could, in the language that calls me, in which
I name desires, the desires which are also fears,
abstractions, generalizations, insecurities,
to form what is unformed, what is chaos, inchoate, or
embryonic, digital, not biologic — though it
does breathe — and how to get to it is to let the coffee
go cold, at least they say that is the way; I tried that way.

∇

Winter, have I lost your thread?
Downwritten whole around you?
I laugh at my poems, scare
my friends, see carefree moments
in the distance, at what cost?
And if I write this backwards,
stay time's goosestep march, with this
superfluous smoke, one more
glass of claret, one fragment
of a poem — all too poor
copy of wild abandon.
Without your thighs to burrow,
I smell the passing age, quick
era passing over me
to where it proudly hurries,
cold of heart. This penmanship
delights in its own decay —
downgraded to scribble, a
palliative effacement,
bathos sutured to my hand.

Winter full of parties I plan to attend and think better.
I'm not pro anything, I'm just speaking. Hear my poems'
pliant snow, trans-white. It's a very long scholarly paper,
but I don't have a stapler. Here I am on stage, what's left?
Now that I'm old enough to be alive, I cant't forget it —
every picture frame hanging askew, floor's slope, every time
out of order, corners joined at odds with corners. Just listen
how I talk to you, without your courage. I was programmed
to be lost — planned incandescence. After Goethe and Spicer,
the word is death, a long line for bread. Like when I'd like to
take my shoes off: I was in the present and the knot wasn't.

∇

How begin after the screen pushed back
as if there's a world to go back to
later? No omens left. Invent them,
throwing forms at glass, whatever sticks.
I can work this stylus in my sleep,
but learn a parole? To map the cracks
of my phone for a way to you? My
Ovid wants to go home, translated,
even if only as a body
for burial. How far that wan world,
and to which end? So sad to be sand,
sad sack; *saudade*. Pity the chair's hard
times under my weight; as the desk must
a vocation make. A young runner
runs by into green identity,
whereas I — barely a graying stone
in the cold's gray manor where I work
on "what is my life?" *It's as if.* Of
course, one can look out a window, one
can float by, remark how one's floating —
dead winter running into winter.

Tuesday: how to go on writing warm words in round rain?
I'd be happy to speak your name in graphic, soundless
verses, but all the O's roll out of reach, so should I
roll there along with them to silence, though I long
to be precise and write you upbeat postcards — "Don't smoke
too much!" etc. — heroically longhanding
every letter or finally install black ribbon
(machine now older than my father was) and bang
thanks and condolences I owe the world that won't
be shut by glass excuses out. Although there is
all this that needs doing, I won't hunker down. Instead
carve open morbid quotation marks into my mind,
not having drunk enough to write a poem, search
my memory for memes and dead men, muse on some
last misunderstanding to find in that old failure
consolation and turn it like old sweaters inside
out in glad animal movements, roll through all things,
un-aging as one's final year, and jester questions
of myself: how is it that winter still hangs on you?

∇

In winter's grip, in malady and warmth —
books at arms reach, but I just scribble,
feign aesthetic undertakings, courting
gout. Apocalyptic nineties poets
spell the end: Stefan Georg, then Rod Smith.
Decadence now retrofolding under
theosophic light of CA's crystals,
fractals stacked. And me, I'm counting coots
with Stebelton by lakeside. They sway
under the shackled sky like ingrown hairs.

With ev'ry year, the highway is encroaching,
closing on the old tow path I pace in
wandering, pastoral and embattled,
against the progress of redundant work.
The novelty of speed wears off in wars
that stretch through generations, carve deeper
old crusade's divides. Though mathematics proves
identity unlikely, we cleave to it
as our last idol, our branded salt, our
special sauce, our soul, while flat worlds on our phones
map blue circles where we stand, as zeros
on the line of numbers in capital's
olympic games. The soma in the water
and the Beatles make it alright. Ice caps melt
while baseball cap couture from China
makes one a living where living's standardized
and standards rise in time with oceans, rent,
and every new day's sun. We've no excuse
for living. Only rail's curvature and bums
are just. Tom Paine was right — why work? Suns set
alike on ghettos and macmansions. Time's
a-wasting. I'd rather not rhetorically

confront you with some searching truth or research
in arrears, when we could sleep till morning, wake,
make love and sleep again, bake pancakes out of
money, raise a glass for ev'ry made mistake
to insulate our bodies against winter.

∇

Unseasonably warm winter's
Sunday, I read the papers,
clowned tiny leisure-class
belonging. Frittered morning
away in frying eggs, head
full of fusty sentences
predicting falling futures.
How one does what one does is now
beyond me. I push against it
from this side of iron gates
and yell, so softly, safely, this
was not meant to be. So let
blond children overrun the park —
I'll seek the castaway bench
in its darkest corner, under
construction, there to fight life,
if life this is, where leaves aren't swept
and the homeless men make do
and paramedics pass blindly
the world made big enough for us.
Here I build my bridge to traverse
the world with a shark's milky eye.

Invisible, I write something
about holding ruddy apples
across my chest, cradled against
wide stripes of garish sweater.
Short of life, a day off. Shapes
pass, mostly soft big people —
slow, save the angular dog
that jumps to the very end
of its master's leash. By sleight
of hand, or miracle, mist rolls
off the disabled fountain.

∇

In a disjunctive age, disconsolate, without connection,
I lick this postage stamp — a thing that you may not have ever licked.
Pulp paper trails the color of cracked walnut shells and cork boards.
To write this is to stay up till tomorrow cannot be a day
to read about the dead, tear further troubles to have later
seams to mend, put forth exhaustion from which to recover, tame
rhetoric in its wide, trembling circus tent. Word for word for word
I change to pass through night in pace with night, time as if bravely
lost, but lost, lost all the same. There's no decision left to make
for those who feared deciding — once, twice, a third, until it was too late;
choice narrows down the lane, in time the brooks and soldiers run away
from tinny villanelles. Even your name, your status update —
divorced, vacating job, collecting dust, disheartened, now deceased —
means little if at all a thing it is to be. Compared to what?
Compared to winter's day? The heat of these laughable plastic keys?

∇

On girders of a bridge, construction's
Cezanne-like line — pained, dark, now trembling,
while distant lights of town blaze moonless
through dark mouths, transparent winter airs.

∇

Pass by the co-work, they offer gelato,
unlimited australian coffee — non-dairy
creamers, sweeteners provided. Check, nothing
quiet's playing at the movies, blue hydrangeas,
so I go home, past runners training behind glass
to run longer in american apparel.
I think I hear somebody say to someone
"You look like a Cy Twombly." Then I come back
to you in Spain, though it's only your photo
I tacked up by the door last winter sometime.

∇

At Heathrow in the morning, the men
move effortlessly baggage carts outside
the rectilinear terminal, draw
dress forms in curving sideways stacks, like
chainlink, hinging in a plastic snake.
So they weave ephemeral cloth. And if
my work might equal this weaving in
grace of purpose... but play upon the keys
of thought has little audible relation
to real singing. There's brushwork turning
in the bristles — a world of likenesses,
imagined limits. Thermodynamic
lawns host painted picnics when the weather's
nice enough, though summer here is not
unlike winter, with clouds of heather wool.

Snakes of steam from winter roofs and potholes
streaming make in these faubourgs an atmosphere,
its cemetery morning lasts all day.
I'm hitting coffee out of the park, lining
up the tasks, like bowling pins, and striking.
Breakfast waits. Into recycling, the journal
with a hundred poets and I the oldest
of those still alive. It'll soon be dark.
I'm heating up my breakfast; the plates drip dry.
What's to be done with day as many grays
as pigeons, chronicles of poor decisions,
whims, fantasies that spin under my needle
feeling for the sounds — it slips to starkness
of the final circle, now tapping slowly
out slow tap of its defeated purpose.

∇

Framed mess of thread, mockery of paint's desire
to resemble, as pained as helplessness
implied in seeing. This difficulty is
also between us, brings intimacy nearer,
breaking mirror. Perhaps regrettable
way out of clauses. Stochastically, I grow
the sequence so that I may lose the way
around the corner, for I give trust too much
to sense, while freedom's to be found in faking
nonsense, blowing on false snow, or permanent
botanicals — forms that have no bearing
on their content, only intensity,
delirious as sex's fleeting image.
Yet, I argue, scream. Color — wet as *a pleat
next Tuesday*, casually ardent at this
copy stand. Pain, as you know, escapes the word;
thus this depravity of sorrow. I have
no information left of you, only
knowledge: forearm, ankle, eyelid — pores, pixels.
Sight deprived of sight in indecision's
unwavering refusal of next winter.

∇

Winter and once more mine is the other guilt.
From sounding syllables, my head is splitting.
All my allotted time it seems I've wasted
on being thorough where no one would notice:
dishes, examining the rain, slowing my prose,
and rounding down the line against my crooked
leaning to fill the void with borrowed rhythms.
Like all others, this book, too, will I regret;
Not for what I missed in order to make time —
for the way it ended.

∇

a twenty in my pocket — from you who felt sorry —
same as $2.22 in frank's pale '58 knuckles.
spent some on a slice (new york temptation) then did some
sulking at the bookstore. it's late and life has not begun.
the sequel's out and i haven't even already seen
planet earth one. leftovers till payday. not really
a job, but i hold it down. almost touched your sleeve, why
would i do that after you told me i was attracted?
denigration is alright, sometimes. let me be a kid
in your arms for an evening in mexico city.
when it's over, say thanks for being around to smile at.
i was around the first time and i'm still around to see
your retrospective. my fellow citizens take care
in visions under daddy's boot — lefties who won't let
their kids read twain, but can't ban ayn rand. yes, history
slides into home — safe — let's have a coke and forget it,
bat at a ball. gnaw on a leg. green hills of iowa
scroll along to their blood conclusions. when asked about
a living wage, they laughed in my face — i felt like david
schubert on the bus through midtown. a poem once a month —
not bad for nonprofit. roll it not fold it. next up,
the cantos, maximus, and all that. as a poet

i'm fortunate to know in the audience tonight says,
fuck everybody — it's more i.r.l. in native mouth;
which is being a poet. rogers & hart they say,
not hart & rogers; who says? typos at our every turn
await the innocent of language. what's foreign when
i am at home, save me? the vinegar soaks up the bad
but not the good, how does it know? sometimes i google
the word *website*. said baraka, "find your self, then kill it,"
which reminds me: denby reading dante's paradiso
as the pills kick in. no rhyme was coming to the mind
and nothing good enough to keep was in the notebooks
when *and the snow blinks down to winter* wrote joan murray.

∇

Here the poet wrote all of mid-winter day
in that brick house, main street of little mill town
in the mountains around the corner from the
bookstore. Wood smoke in the air, low clouds, low-
lying sun caught up in lower branches, like
its lowered gaze, that bare melancholy of
identification. Such long days are
no longer long; can a coal century bear
its weight in wars and prose? Umbrish gardens
of the twilight of the gods, these hills, these
mansions turning downward at the lip. This is
my house, I've lived in it, made love, looked out
these windows, baked in the kitchen, misshaped love
by feeding one lover's cake to another.

Had I your hands, I'd give up my ambitions.
What matters now that far away you think
of nothing but what's close at hand? To win
your pity, that it congrue to mercy
is my burden; to speak it burdens others.
This posture gets the worst of me, the better
to walk your mile in my shoes and get nowhere.
Somewhere winds a clock, I hear its grinding
gears, its bells in empty tower of my chest.
Say "ancestors" — they'll sigh alright. Drink until
insight comes, or sleep. What's liquid must pour out
and vessel empty of what memories
a friend to lend a hand: penitent, gloveless,
sweeping snow from our last winter's windshield.

∇

Winter — a landscape in questions, old
punctuation. The floorboards creaking,
I step out to bitter moons. Don't worry,
the notebooks are all with the proper
authorities. Such little things make life
and buttonholes let it seep out. It can
happen in no time and now it's over.
The window cracks the landscape into
allegory. The grove of spruce or pine,
over there, it stands apart. The planner
is full, and it's only February.

First off, I am the worst there is on earth. Back there, the light
shone on the vernacular as in the middle of my life
I came upon myself in wood one dark, protracted evening
of rubbing some ideas together. Rushed back for solace,
solitude with one barely known to me who wears my glasses
as if to clearly see what seems too far to see, too hard,
and other times, too close, too easy. Ease of positions:
Our shit ain't their shit, etc. Whatever works for you
beyond suppositions, under the givens of things being
things, as if individuated. No time to write this, so
wake up, smell coffee on the wind, and everyone's speaking
Ravickian. I got alerts a few days late. No one
was told about the curfew in Kafr Qassem. So this is
dispersal? Or spread 'em, like ashes. I'd call poetry
tomorrow, but it's out for the day of the dead. Offered help
leads straight to dropped the plastic salad spinner. Was what you heard
lip service to the fugitives from capital's endowed chair?
Cut to a turn too soon and you're rolling over. You can
always be right, if you like that sort of feeling pretty-mouthed.
Missed Bernadette's show — now it's someone else's memory
moved from paper to product-oriented magma. I was
accused of sensing, but it was trans-sensual. Foreigners

speak what may only be hinted. What's not to be missed is life,

but that too, round as midnight — at the count of three, it's gone —

one sees it with one's ear and winter's never far from water.

Next day the world begins again, full sun
in the room can't read the scribbling of late
last night once all had left and sleep swept down
sudden, nor brush nor water on the face.
Electric toothbrush could have saved you once —
now it's too late, as one who would have loved
you had you brighter teeth is on a bright
journey, in stronger arms than your arms could
have strength, et cetera. There are so many
twists — as creases in the sheets, pocks in brick —
in fate. Eyes weary, obliged to write: you have
misunderstood me, you who once joyed at this
touch... How sweet — last cigarette at gallows,
at the wall; born to die how many times,
the twenty-fifth day of the month December
in droll satire's laughter, in a game
of truths and lies (what need distinguish them
in the biography — as many I's
as sleep through mornings, not enough, come typing,
come what may). The puce of prisms, windows
at certain slant of light, some things egged on
by electricity to hum. My shadow

on the floor to check the sentimental tear,
next to a peel of garlic on the rutted
parquet, next to grays, and lists, lists endlessly
repeating in endlessly retreating worlds.
Guests and ghosts of guests outreach for coffee,
forget their scarves to pick up later on,
as I search for the honorary plaque,
for tombs to what will be forgotten yet
remains where lies last winter's fallen snow.

Remember winter chapbooks
and long days of chairs being
chairs under us, as usual,
useable, useful as the guilt
of "Remember, I did this
for you." Sweeping the floor in
anticipation of your
midnight visit, I'm doing it
for me as much as you and think
how terrible to mention
in the future, *remember*...
I'd rather say it's for me
& my boring blue notebook,
meanest of my small possessions.
Surely this smoke will clear my head.
Offer my cig to the set sun,
ash on the floor I just swept.

What survives winter? Under spell
of Stein, swept so much under
the rug, see the bump rising up,
a raised belly. I blew smoke

in your face for you and you
and I wrote about letters
& addressees, remember?
The strangest people remember
my poems, but friends rarely do.
Not that I remember all
of yours (and glad you didn't
do me that favor). Turns out love
doesn't read you, doesn't listen
when you talk whatever you talk,
doesn't care much for pain as yours
is a part of it, like a chair
or other *already things*.

I balked at winter as a child,
drank deeply of a different mud.
Now more alone, I drink low light
and wait — it's almost midnight —
for snow to dress up night? Ah,
melancholy. It's time to scrap
a bit, complain, waste time, forget
enigmas, eventually

stupid ends, and supermen,

their proud memento mori.

What have I learned from you, poem?

With steady hand, I "move to trash."

What hope of whispers when evening

is broadcast. Reduced to traces,

stray fluids on temporary

surfaces; yet once he could

recite the Aeneid backward.

To have a book to read and not
to read it. Smoke out a window
at the rain — someone to talk to
but not to talk with them. Silence
but for plastic keys struck softly.
No bell for waking, nor for sleep;
tolling the eights on chestnut desk.
Who will continue here once roads
are open after winter's close?

Acknowledgements

Many thanks to the editors of *BOMB Magazine, The Brooklyn Rail, Caesura, Chicago Review, Poetry at Sangam, SAND* (Berlin), *Verse, Vestiges* (Black Sun Lit), and *Zaza*, where several of these poems originally appeared. The poem beginning "Winter comes calling while I'm on / vacation..." was printed by Emily Larned as a broadside inserted into the limited-edition chapbook *From a Winter Notebook* (Alder & Frankia, 2021).

Though most of these poems employ the work of others, translated or transformed, there are several here that contain unattributed wholesale appropriations of lines or phrases — appearing in italics — from poems by Mel Elberg, Alan Gilbert, Thom Jurek, Stephen Rodefer, and Keith Waldrop; my apologies and thanks to these poets.

FONO
GRAF

OTHER FONOGRAF ED. TITLES

Fonograf Editions is a registered 501(c)(3) non-profit organization. Find more information about the press at: fonografeditions.com.